Spiral of Sensations

In the stillness of the night,
Whispers dance on the breeze,
Moonlight bathes the quiet streets,
Heartbeats echo with ease.

Colors swirl in the morning sun,
A gentle touch awakens dreams,
Laughter floats like petals down,
Life is brighter than it seems.

Moments linger, soft and sweet,
Fingertips brush against the skin,
Every sigh a melody,
Each glance a secret to begin.

Time weaves tales with silken thread,
A tapestry of joy and pain,
In every fold, a story read,
The spiral turns, love's refrain.

Beneath the Surface

Beneath the waves, a world unfolds,
Whispers of secrets, stories untold.
Echoes of currents, shadows that play,
Life pulses gently, in hues of gray.

Coral gardens, vibrant and bright,
Dance with the fish, in shimmering light.
Bubbles rise softly, like dreams from the deep,
Where silence and wonder, together they sleep.

Tranquil Turbulence

Stillness breaks, a gentle sigh,
Ripples of calm, beneath the sky.
Clouds swirl softly, a dance of delight,
Peace interwoven with the rush of the night.

Waves whisper secrets, in rhythmic embrace,
Heartbeats echo, finding their place.
Nature's orchestra, a soothing refrain,
Harmony rising, like whispers of rain.

Colors of the Heart

Scarlet and gold, emotions collide,
Brushstrokes of passion, in colors we hide.
Azure of dreams, where hope takes flight,
Emerald whispers, in the dappled light.

Violet shadows, where fears often dwell,
Painted with stories, we long to tell.
A canvas of feelings, forever we share,
Each hue a reminder, of love's gentle care.

A Journey Within

Footsteps echo, down halls of the mind,
Searching for treasures, in shadows we find.
Rooms filled with memories, laughter, and tears,
Whispers of visions, over the years.

Mirrors reflect, the hopes that we chase,
Futures unfolding, with time and with grace.
A tapestry woven, of dreams made of light,
In the journey within, our spirits ignite.

Reflections in the Rain

Puddles shimmer on the street,
Mirrored dreams beneath my feet.
Raindrops dance in soft embrace,
Nature's tears leave gentle trace.

Clouds whisper secrets, gray and light,
Every droplet, pure delight.
Lost in thought, I drift away,
In the rain, I find my play.

Moments in the Moonlight

Silver beams on waters glow,
Painting shadows, ebb and flow.
Whispers float on evening air,
Moonlit secrets everywhere.

Holding breath as night unfolds,
Stories that the darkness holds.
Time stands still, the world at ease,
In this moment, I am free.

A Portrait of Yearning

Brushstrokes of a heart's desire,
Color dreams that lift me higher.
Every hue a tale untold,
Yearning whispers, soft and bold.

Canvas wide, I lose my way,
In the art of yesterday.
Drawn to futures yet to come,
A portrait waits, the beat of drum.

Waves of Wonder

Crest and trough, the ocean's dance,
Mysteries in every glance.
Salt and spray, the world anew,
In each wave, a dream breaks through.

Tides pull at the heart's own shore,
Echoes of a longing core.
Endless journeys, wide and grand,
Waves of wonder, hand in hand.

Enchantment of Empathy

In shadows deep, we find the light,
A whispered word, a shared delight.
Hearts intertwined, we lift the veil,
Together we rise, together we sail.

Gentle eyes that see the soul,
In every tear, we make each whole.
A silent bond, a tender grace,
In every smile, a warm embrace.

Palette of Passion

Crimson dreams on canvas bright,
Brushstrokes dance with pure delight.
Colors swirl, emotions flow,
In every hue, a tale to show.

Fires burn where hearts ignite,
The rhythm sways in moonlit night.
With every heartbeat, love unfolds,
A masterpiece that life beholds.

Storms of Solitude

Winds howl loud, the silence breaks,
In quiet corners, a heart aches.
Whispers echo where shadows creep,
In solitude's grip, memories sleep.

Thunder roars, the skies turn gray,
Yet in the chaos, we find our way.
A tranquil storm, a tempest's grace,
In solitude's arms, we find our place.

Pulses of Connection

In every gaze, a spark ignites,
A dance unseen in silent nights.
Fingers brush like summer rain,
In tides of truth, we break the chain.

With every laugh, our spirits soar,
An open door to something more.
In every heartbeat, we feel the tie,
As pulses sync beneath the sky.

Luminous Sentiments

In whispers soft, the stars do gleam,
They dance in shadows, weave a dream.
Each twinkle tells a heart's desire,
A glow ignites the fading fire.

Moonlit beams on paths untold,
Adventures wait for brave and bold.
With every pulse, a story spun,
In radiant light, our souls are one.

Palette of Dreams

Colors drip from visions bright,
Brushes dance in gentle light.
A canvas stretched on sky's embrace,
Where hues of love find endless space.

With every stroke, a tale unfurls,
A symphony of swirls and whirls.
In vivid shades of hope we blend,
A masterpiece that knows no end.

Chasing the Unseen

Through misty veils, we tread the path,
In search of echoes, lost in wrath.
The silence calls, a haunting song,
Where shadows play and dreams belong.

With every step, the heart takes flight,
In realms of dusk, beyond the light.
We chase the whispers on the breeze,
Unlocking secrets with such ease.

Threads of Longing

In woven strands of fate we find,
A tapestry that's gently lined.
Each thread a pulse, a soft caress,
Binding souls in sweet duress.

Through time and space, the fibers weave,
In every knot, the heart believes.
A fabric rich with love's design,
In threads of longing, we entwine.

Crescendo of Care

In gentle whispers, hearts align,
Each gesture soft, a thread divine.
With open hands, we share our light,
Together we will face the night.

A swell of kindness in each tone,
United voices, never alone.
Through trials faced and laughter shared,
In every moment, love declared.

In storms we weather, courage grows,
A harmony that ever flows.
Bound by trust, we rise and dare,
A symphony of hope and care.

The world may dim, and shadows play,
But love's bright notes will guide the way.
In every heartbeat, dreams take flight,
A crescendo of care ignites the night.

Melodies of the Mind

In silence deep, our thoughts will dance,
A rhythm flows, a fleeting chance.
Within the stillness, dreams arise,
Unfolding secrets, veils in disguise.

Each memory a note, well played,
A symphony where dreams cascade.
With whispers soft as twilight falls,
We weave our tales through life's great halls.

In moments cherished, wisdom sings,
A harmony that hopefulness brings.
Through echoes of both joy and pain,
The melodies of life remain.

With open hearts, we find the keys,
Unlocking depths with gentle ease.
In every mind, a song to find,
These melodies, our souls entwined.

The Fire of Empathy

In every heart, a flame ignites,
A warmth that dances through the nights.
With every story shared and told,
A fire of care that never cold.

Through trials faced, we stand as one,
A blazing strength, two hearts now spun.
Each tear we shed, a spark embraced,
In unity, our fears erased.

Compassion's light will guide our way,
Illuminating shadows, day by day.
In every struggle, we find our place,
The fire of empathy, a warm embrace.

Together strong, we rise anew,
In every sigh, compassion's true.
The world transformed with every spark,
In love's bright fire, we leave our mark.

Portraits of Peace

In every moment, stillness calls,
Through gentle winds, or quiet halls.
Each brushstroke soft, each hue so kind,
Portraits of peace that hearts can find.

Together weaving dreams so bright,
With laughter shared, we chase the light.
A tapestry of hope unfurled,
In shades of love, we paint the world.

In silence, beauty finds its place,
As empathy unveils its grace.
Through open hearts, we seek the source,
Portraits of peace, our steadfast course.

With every breath, a promise made,
To build a world where kindness stays.
In every soul, a canvas wide,
Where portraits of peace forever bide.

Whispers of the Soul's Essence

In the silence, secrets blend,
Softly spoken, hearts descend.
Echoes linger, shadows play,
Whispers guide us, come what may.

In depths unseen, the truth reveals,
Tender moments, the spirit heals.
Voices gentle, soft as air,
In dreams we dance, united there.

Kaleidoscope of Emotions

Colors flash in vivid sight,
Joy and sorrow, day and night.
Each hue tells a vibrant tale,
In this rhythm, we prevail.

Swirls of laughter, tears that shine,
Melodies that intertwine.
An ever-changing canvas flows,
In this journey, feeling grows.

Heartbeats in Twilight

As daylight fades, the stars awake,
Whispers linger, night's embrace.
Gentle moments, pulse of time,
In twilight's calm, the soul climbs.

Rhythms echo, soft and slow,
In the dark, our heartbeats glow.
A symphony beneath the moon,
We find solace, sweet cocoon.

Ethereal Threads of Memory

Fleeting whispers, threads so fine,
Stitching moments, yours and mine.
In the fabric, stories weave,
Eternal bonds we shall achieve.

Fragments dance in the warm light,
Holding close, the heart takes flight.
Each remembrance, bright and true,
In this tapestry, me and you.

Dance of the Inner Light

In the stillness of the night,
Whispers of the heart take flight.
Twinkling stars, they guide the way,
In dreams where shadows softly play.

A rhythm beats within the soul,
Each movement makes the spirit whole.
With every turn, the world does gleam,
In the dance where we dare to dream.

Spectrum of Silent Sighs

Colors weave in quiet grace,
Every hue a soft embrace.
Silent sighs that fill the air,
Echoes of a heart laid bare.

Through each shade, emotions blend,
Promises that never end.
In the spectrum, find your peace,
In silence, let your worries cease.

Echoes of Unseen Desires

Beyond the veil of what is seen,
Lie the dreams that dare to glean.
In every thought, a touch of gold,
Whispers of the brave and bold.

Yearnings pulse beneath the skin,
Calling forth the light within.
Echoes dance in shadows deep,
Awakening secrets we keep.

Chasing Stars Through Shadows

Beneath the canopy of night,
We chase the stars, igniting light.
Through shadows that stretch wide and far,
With hopes aligned like distant stars.

Each step a journey, fierce and bright,
Illuminating paths of right.
In every heartbeat, dreams arise,
Chasing stars through endless skies.

Heartstrings in Harmony

In twilight's gentle embrace, we meet,
Melodies linger, bittersweet.
Two souls dance in a perfect tune,
Underneath the silver moon.

Together we weave our dreams,
Like fleeting whispers, love redeems.
Every note a heartbeat's grace,
In this sacred, timeless space.

With every chord, our spirits soar,
An echo of what came before.
Bound by strings, our laughter sings,
In harmony, the heartstrings cling.

Through life's ebb and flow we glide,
Hand in hand, side by side.
In this symphony, we find our way,
Love's refrain, forever stays.

A Symphony of Sighs

In shadows deep, the silence weaves,
A tale of loss that softly leaves.
Each sigh a note, a longing call,
Echoes whisper through the hall.

The heart plays softly, a quiet song,
In memories where we belong.
Each breath a phrase, each tear a rhyme,
Caught in the web of fleeting time.

With every sigh, a story's spun,
From dawn's first light to set of sun.
A symphony of what we miss,
Captured in time, sealed with a kiss.

Yet in the hush, hope still resides,
A gentle warmth that never hides.
Through every sorrow, joy survives,
In the music of our lives.

Radiant Reflections

In morning light, the world awakes,
Mirrored dreams in tranquil lakes.
Colors bloom in soft embrace,
Nature's canvas, a sacred space.

With each dawn, a story told,
A tapestry of hopes we hold.
From shadows cast to brilliance bright,
Reflections dance in golden light.

Every moment, a fleeting glance,
In beauty found, we find our chance.
The heart, a vessel of endless hue,
Where radiant dreams come shining through.

Embrace the light, let spirits rise,
In every heartbeat, the world lies.
Together, we paint the skies so wide,
In radiant reflections, love will bide.

Solstice of the Spirit

Amidst the changing tides we stand,
In seasons marked by nature's hand.
A solstice calling, whispering near,
Awakening dreams, banishing fear.

The sun dips low, the shadows blend,
In twilight's grace, the day will end.
But in this pause, let souls ignite,
A flicker of hope, a guiding light.

With every dusk, new stars will bloom,
Dispelling darkness, chasing gloom.
The spirit dances, wild and free,
In the embrace of destiny.

In unity, we find our way,
Through night's embrace toward a new day.
Let every heart, a beacon's flare,
Guide us onward, beyond despair.

Abundant Affections

In the garden of dreams, we bloom,
Colors shifting, dispelling gloom.
Whispers dance on a gentle breeze,
Love's embrace, a sweet tease.

Underneath the starry night,
Hearts entwined, a wondrous sight.
Laughter echoes, bright and clear,
Companions lost, yet always near.

Every glance, a silent vow,
Seasons change, but still we're now.
Time may fade, yet love will thrill,
A tapestry, woven still.

In every touch, the warmth ignites,
Fires glowing on the coldest nights.
Abundant affections softly sway,
Guiding us, come what may.

A Corsage of Emotion

Petals soft, in colors bright,
Adorning hearts with pure delight.
A corsage woven with our dreams,
Fragile threads in golden beams.

Moments captured, fragile grace,
In every smile, a warm embrace.
Together in this dance we move,
Crafting stories, hearts the groove.

Each memory, a fragrant bloom,
Filling spaces, chasing gloom.
In the rhythm of love's tune,
We find solace, like the moon.

Worn close to the heart, we share,
Every joy, and every care.
A corsage of emotion glows,
In the light where true love flows.

Soft Cries of Courage

In the shadows where fears reside,
Soft cries whisper, brave the tide.
With every tear, a strength revealed,
Courage grows, pain is healed.

Through the valleys, dark and deep,
Voices rise, awakening sleep.
In the silence, we stand tall,
Together we rise, we will not fall.

Wounds may ache, yet hearts will mend,
Stronger bonds, on love depend.
Soft cries echo, breaking free,
In our hearts, hope's decree.

Every challenge, a chance to soar,
With every battle, we seek more.
Soft cries of courage, loud and clear,
Unite us all, banish fear.

Hues of the Heart

In the canvas of our days,
Colors merge in endless ways.
From gentle pastels to bold shores,
The hues of the heart constantly pours.

Sunset whispers in shades of gold,
Stories within, splendidly told.
Each stroke a moment, bright and rare,
In the gallery of love laid bare.

Blues of sorrow, reds of fire,
Every hue reflects desire.
With every heartbeat, the lines define,
A masterpiece, forever thine.

In the art of us, we find peace,
A spectrum where all colors cease.
Hues of the heart paint our skies,
In love's embrace, our spirits rise.

Mosaic of Memories

Fragments of time, in pieces they lay,
Whispers of laughter, in shadows they play.
Colors of joy, in vibrant display,
Crafting a story, that won't fade away.

Fleeting moments, like fireflies glow,
A dance of the past, in the twilight's flow.
Each tile a heartbeat, a tale to bestow,
Mosaic of memories, in hearts we sow.

Echoes of voices, floating in air,
Tales of togetherness, precious and rare.
Together we wandered, without a care,
In this rich tapestry, our love laid bare.

Cherished embrace, where time stands still,
A journey we've traveled, with heart and will.
In this mosaic, our love's the quill,
Writing forever, our dreams to fulfill.

Alchemy of Affection

In the cauldron of heart, emotions collide,
Mixing the laughter with tears that abide.
A sprinkle of hope, and love as a guide,
In this alchemy's magic, two souls will bide.

Moments like gold, transformed in the flame,
A bond forged in fire, never the same.
With each tender glance, we play the same game,
In the alchemy of affection, love's the name.

Soft whispers at dusk, as shadows convene,
Infinite secrets, in twilight unseen.
With every heartbeat, a promise serene,
In the potion of us, forever we're keen.

Woven together, by hands intertwined,
A spell of connection, two hearts aligned.
This alchemy's treasure, in love we find,
Crafting our future, uniquely designed.

Secrets of Serendipity

In the quiet moments, chance takes a seat,
Whispers of fate, where lovers first meet.
Unexpected journeys, with paths so sweet,
In the secrets of serendipity, hearts skip a beat.

A glance across rooms, a spark in the air,
Destined encounters, through brush of a hair.
Moments unplanned, we find everywhere,
In the dance of the cosmos, love's the affair.

Twists of the universe, weaves stories anew,
In shadows of fate, we wander and pursue.
Through laughter and trials, together we grew,
Unraveling secrets, in all that we do.

In the tapestry woven, with threads of delight,
Serendipity's kiss brings joy to the night.
Hand in hand journey, our dreams take flight,
In this secret of love, the world's shining bright.

Tapestry of the Heart

Threads of emotion, so vividly spun,
Stitch by stitch, we weave till we're one.
Colors of passion, in the radiant sun,
In this tapestry of the heart, love has begun.

Patterns of laughter, with edges of tears,
Memories gathered, through all of the years.
Together we journey, no need for our fears,
In the fabric of life, our love perseveres.

Dappled with dreams, in a rich array,
Every heartbeat whispers what words cannot say.
In the loom of time, our spirits in play,
Crafting a story, that won't fade away.

Each thread a promise, each knot a decree,
In the tapestry woven, forever we'll be.
Bound by affection, so wild and so free,
In the heart's great design, it's you and it's me.

Gazes that Ignite

In a crowded room, eyes meet,
Silent sparks dance, a heartbeat.
Flames flicker, passion ignites,
Two souls connect, in soft lights.

Whispers linger in the air,
Promises murmured, unaware.
A single glance, worlds collide,
In that moment, love won't hide.

Unseen forces pull them close,
With every look, their hearts do boast.
In the depth of soulful gaze,
They find solace, endless blaze.

Lost in time, the world fades out,
In their gaze, no room for doubt.
A bond ignites, fierce and bright,
Together dancing, day and night.

Threads of Timelessness

Weaving dreams through space and time,
Golden threads in patterns rhyme.
Moments stitched in gentle care,
Echoes linger in the air.

Stories spun from whispered tales,
In every heart, a love prevails.
Through the years, we stand entwined,
A tapestry of souls aligned.

Time may drift, yet we remain,
Bound by joy, anchored in pain.
Each memory a colored strand,
Framed within a tender hand.

In this fabric, rich and vast,
The essence of us, forever cast.
Through every tear and laugh we share,
Threads of timelessness, pure and rare.

Resonance of Intuition

In the quiet, whispers call,
Intuition's dance, we feel it all.
A gentle nudge, the heart's own guide,
Leading us where truths abide.

Moments linger, paths unfold,
Secrets hidden, waiting bold.
A knowing glance, we trust the flow,
In resonance, our spirits grow.

Softly speaking, feelings rise,
Inner voices, no disguise.
In the stillness, wisdom speaks,
Through every joy, through every peak.

Embrace the magic, heed the call,
Intuition leads, we shall not fall.
With each heartbeat, we align,
Trust the journey; the stars will shine.

A Voyage of Emotions

Sailing forth on waves of dreams,
Emotions swell like moonlit beams.
Each tide brings whispers, soft and low,
Navigating through joy and woe.

Currents pull, the heart's own sail,
With every heartbeat, we set our trail.
Storms may rise, yet we'll stay true,
Guided by stars, in skies so blue.

In the depths of laughter, tears,
We find our strength, confront our fears.
Together, we chart the unknown,
In every heartbeat, love has grown.

Through the horizon, shadows play,
In this voyage, we find our way.
Emotions dance as we embrace,
A journey shared, a sacred space.

Unraveled Yearnings

In the depths of quiet night,
Whispers dance like softest light.
Dreams unfold, a fragile thread,
Tales of love that linger, spread.

Hands that reach but never touch,
Hopes that bloom but not too much.
Hearts that ache with sweet despair,
Yearning lingers in the air.

Time moves slowly, shadows creep,
In the silence, secrets seep.
Voices murmur from the past,
Echoes of a love that last.

Wishes tossed upon the breeze,
Finding solace in the trees.
Unraveled threads of what could be,
In the heart, they still run free.

Rapture in Silence

Underneath the silver moon,
Softest sighs create a tune.
In stillness, hearts begin to dance,
Lost in love's enchanting trance.

Stars above begin to shine,
Each one whispers, you are mine.
In the hush, our souls collide,
Embracing love we cannot hide.

Moments linger, time stands still,
In these hours, I feel the thrill.
A gentle breeze, a lover's breath,
Connecting hearts beyond all death.

In the silence, rapture grows,
Where the secret river flows.
Together, we will find our way,
In the night, forever stay.

Celestial Touch

Stardust kisses on the skin,
Whispers of the night begin.
Heaven's spark ignites the soul,
In your gaze, I find my whole.

Floating through the cosmic skies,
In the hush, our spirits rise.
Every heartbeat sings a song,
Where the lost and found belong.

Through the vastness, we embark,
Chasing shadows in the dark.
Fingers trace the endless light,
In this dance, we spark the night.

Galaxies within our hearts,
Every breath, a work of art.
Touched by grace, we intertwine,
In the cosmos, love will shine.

Eclipsed Sentiments

When the world bows in the dark,
Silent echoes leave a mark.
In the shadows, feelings loom,
Whispers echo from the gloom.

Tides of passion rise and fall,
Yet in silence, we hear the call.
Cloaked in mystery's embrace,
Lost, yet found in love's warm space.

Faded stars await their cue,
In the stillness, thoughts feel new.
Eclipsed by doubts, but never lost,
In love's light, we bear the cost.

Hearts entwined, our fate is sealed,
In the quiet, truths revealed.
Even in the darkest night,
Eclipsed feelings ignite the light.

Sentient Landscapes

Mountains whisper ancient tales,
Rivers hum in rhythmic scales.
Trees sway gently, minds they share,
Each blade of grass shows hidden care.

Clouds dance softly in the breeze,
Painting skies with effortless ease.
Every stone has stories old,
Nature's essence, rich and bold.

Winds carry dreams upon their wings,
In every corner, life still sings.
From valleys deep to peaks so high,
The world around us breathes and sighs.

In harmony, these forms align,
Crafting moments, pure and fine.
Sentient landscapes, vast and true,
Awake their spirit, just for you.

The Weaving of Wishes

Threads of hope in twilight's loom,
Stitching dreams in shades of gloom.
Whispers travel on the night,
Bringing forth the softest light.

Each wish cast into the stars,
Pulses brightly, near and far.
Woven hearts entwined with care,
Fleeting moments, sweet and rare.

In silken strands, our hopes abound,
In the quiet, magic's found.
Embroidered tales of love and grace,
The weaving binds time and space.

With every knot, a story spun,
In the fabric, we are one.
Wishes dance, a vibrant hue,
In the tapestry of me and you.

Whirls of Warmth

Embers flicker with a soft glow,
As dusk settles, time moves slow.
Hearts entwined in gentle plays,
Whispers shared in twilight's maze.

In the cozy, warmth surrounds,
Love encircles, joy abounds.
Laughter lingers in the air,
Every moment, sweetly shared.

Cider sips and fireside dreams,
Life's simple joys like flowing streams.
Each embrace, a spark to ignite,
Whirls of warmth on winter nights.

In the stillness, souls will blend,
A magic that will never end.
Holding close what we can find,
In whirls of warmth, we unwind.

Flickers of Insight

In shadows deep, a light appears,
A whispering truth calms our fears.
Moments pause to gently teach,
Flickers of insight, within reach.

Through quiet contemplation's gaze,
The mind unfurls, in a haze.
Wisdom sprouts like springtime blooms,
Opening hearts in shadowed rooms.

Connections weave, a sacred thread,
In the stillness, thoughts are fed.
Each flicker ignites the spark,
Guiding souls out of the dark.

With open hearts, we start to see,
The beauty in your mystery.
Flickers of insight, bright and clear,
Illuminate what we hold dear.

Serenade of Hidden Hues

Whispers dance in twilight's glow,
Colors blend where dreams once flow.
A palette made of secret sighs,
Crafted beneath the endless skies.

Each shade a tale of hearts that yearn,
In shadows cast, the lanterns burn.
With every brush, a moment caught,
In silence woven, love is sought.

Through the night, the canvas sings,
Of hopes that bloom on fragile wings.
While moonlight strokes the painted space,
A serenade of heartfelt grace.

Veil of Joy and Sorrow

Life's a tapestry, woven tight,
Threads of laughter, strands of night.
Beneath the veil, emotions twine,
In joy's embrace, in sorrow's line.

The heart's a stage for every scene,
In echoes soft, where we've been.
With every tear, a lesson learned,
A longing deep, a passion burned.

Yet through the mist, the sun will rise,
A dance of shadows, light implies.
In intertwined, the truth displayed,
In joy and sorrow, love's cascade.

Flickering Flames of Longing

In twilight's breath, a flame ignites,
Flickers soft, through whispered nights.
Desires spark, in shadows dance,
A silent call, a fleeting chance.

With every glow, a heartbeat's plea,
In warmth entwined, a mystery.
The sparks of dreams, they rise and fall,
In every ember, hear the call.

Yet winds may shift, the flames may fade,
But in the glow, our hopes are laid.
To chase the night, to brave the dark,
A flickering flame, a burning spark.

Tide of Unexpressed Thoughts

A sea of words, unspoken dreams,
Rising waves in silent streams.
Thoughts like tides, they ebb and flow,
In quiet depths, the heart's shadow.

Each pulse a wish, a whisper lost,
In hidden depths, the tempest tossed.
Visions swirl in ocean's sway,
Chasing the sun, the light of day.

Yet in the depths, a truth does dwell,
Where unexpressed has stories to tell.
In the swell of thoughts, we find our way,
Through the tide of dreams, we long to stay.

Solstice of the Heart

In the glow of fading light,
We find warmth in the chill,
Seasons shift with whispered dreams,
As time begins to stand still.

Through shadows that softly creep,
The sun dances on the edge,
Echoes of love painted bright,
In a twilight they pledge.

Holding close the memories,
Of laughter and gentle sighs,
The heartbeat of a moment,
As the shortest day flies.

Let us gather all our hopes,
Beneath a sky of deep blue,
In the solstice, hearts awake,
Embracing what is true.

Enchantment in Every Tear

Every tear that glistens bright,
Holds a world of silent songs,
The weight of joys and sorrows,
Where every heart truly longs.

In the cracks of broken dreams,
Lives a beauty like the dawn,
With each drop, a soft whisper,
Of hopes yet to be drawn.

Through the veil of anguish deep,
Resilience blooms like a flower,
In the garden of the soul,
It finds strength in its power.

With every tear, a story shared,
An enchantment softly sewn,
In the fabric of our being,
We are never alone.

Colors of Untold Dreams

In the canvas of the night,
Brush strokes of the heart collide,
Colors dance with wild delight,
Where every fear can hide.

The hues of passion, pain, and joy,
Merge in a fleeting embrace,
Each dream a glimmering toy,
In the vast, star-studded space.

With every shade, a story breathes,
Silently yearning to share,
The palette of our wishes,
Floating on the evening air.

In this mosaic of the soul,
We find the art of our schemes,
In every heart's whispered call,
Lie colors of untold dreams.

Embrace of the Unfathomable

In the depths where shadows play,
Lies a whisper, dark and deep,
An embrace that pulls away,
Yet beckons us to leap.

The unfathomable calls our name,
A murmur, soft, yet so loud,
In silence, we feel the same,
Embraced by the waiting shroud.

Through fears that curl like smoke,
We dare to step into the night,
With every heartache evoked,
In the darkness, we find light.

So let us dance with shadows bold,
In the realms of what we seek,
For in the unknown, stories unfold,
In the unfathomable, we speak.

Echoes of Euphoria

In the dawn, whispers light,
Dancing dreams take their flight.
Laughter spills like morning dew,
In the warmth, hearts feel anew.

Chasing shadows, we entwine,
Every moment, pure and divine.
Joy cascades like gentle rain,
Echoes linger, sweet refrain.

Colors burst in vibrant hues,
Every heartbeat sings the blues.
In this realm of endless bliss,
We find solace in the kiss.

Life's a song, a tender tune,
Underneath the playful moon.
Euphoria's gentle embrace,
In our hearts, we find our place.

Tides of Emotion

Waves surge in the night sky,
Pulling dreams as they drift by.
Hearts like oceans rise and fall,
In their depths, we heed the call.

Whispers of the restless sea,
Carrying thoughts that set us free.
Calming tides bring inner peace,
As the storm begins to cease.

Gentle rhythms, soft and slow,
Every ebb, a chance to grow.
Along the shore of hope we stand,
With open hearts, hand in hand.

In the currents, we find grace,
Embrace the change, the wild chase.
Through the depths, our spirits roam,
In every wave, we find our home.

Veils of Introspection

In the silence, shadows creep,
Through the mind, the secrets seep.
Layered thoughts, a quiet dance,
In still moments, we take a chance.

Mirrored faces blur and fade,
Lost in mists, truths masquerade.
Peeling back the tender veils,
In our heart, the wisdom pales.

Questions linger in the air,
Searching deep, we lay bare.
Embracing all that seems unclear,
In the flow, we conquer fear.

Through the labyrinth, we will tread,
Finding paths where angels fled.
In the stillness, echoes call,
With each step, we rise or fall.

Dance of the Soul

In the twilight, shadows sway,
Rhythms join the night and day.
Every heartbeat, syncopates,
In this space, our spirits celebrate.

Whirling under starlit grace,
Each movement finds its own place.
In this dance of pure delight,
Souls ignite in the gentle night.

Laughter twirls, and sorrows fade,
Every twirl, a promise made.
Lost in time, we all belong,
In the dance, we find our song.

Circles form with endless flow,
As the unity starts to grow.
Together in this sacred role,
We become the dance of the soul.

Sails of the Heart's Voyage

In whispers soft, we set our course,
Through waves of dreams, with gentle force.
The horizon calls, a beckoning light,
Our hearts like sails, ready for flight.

The wind it dances, around our oars,
Each heartbeat echoes, and gently soars.
Together we navigate, the vast unknown,
In every moment, our love has grown.

With stars above, and moon's embrace,
We chart our path, this sacred space.
From port to port, we drift and sway,
In the sea of love, we find our way.

So lift the anchor, let the journey start,
With every wave, we'll share our heart.
For in this voyage, a truth rings clear,
Together forever, my dear, my dear.

Reflections of a Gentle Storm

Clouds gather softly upon the ground,
A symphony whispers, without a sound.
Raindrops caress the thirsty earth,
In each beating heart, a quiet rebirth.

The winds weave tales of love and despair,
In the gentle storm, we find repair.
Lightning flickers, a fleeting spark,
Illuminating dreams that dance in the dark.

Amidst the chaos, solace is found,
In swirling memories, we are bound.
Each droplet falling, a story unfolds,
In the embrace of nature, our truth holds.

Wrapped in the tempest, we find our peace,
As the gentle storm grants us release.
In the storm's embrace, together we'll stand,
Guided by love, hand in hand.

Cradle of Yearning

In the stillness of night, dreams take flight,
Yearning for whispers that feel so right.
Stars twinkle softly in velvet skies,
Cradling desires with tender sighs.

The moonlight bathes the world in grace,
Each shadow dances, a warm embrace.
In the cradle of longing, our hearts collide,
A timeless connection that can't be denied.

With every heartbeat, our souls ignite,
An infinite journey, a dance of light.
Through the valleys of hope, we wander free,
In this cradle, just you and me.

So let the night weave its magic spell,
In the silence, we find all is well.
For in our yearning, a truth we see,
Together forever, eternally.

Luminous Lullabies of the Mind

Softly the night spills its luminous dreams,
Lullabies echo in silver beams.
In whispers gentle, the story unfurls,
A tapestry woven with stardust pearls.

Through midnight thoughts, our spirits take flight,
In symphonies whispered, we find our light.
The mind cradles visions, vivid and bright,
In this gentle dance, we embrace the night.

Each lullaby carries a promise so sweet,
Of love everlasting, a rhythmic beat.
In the depths of our dreams, we find our way,
Guided by starlight that will never sway.

So as stars twinkle, we hold them near,
In luminous lullabies, we conquer fear.
For in the embrace of the quiet divine,
Our hearts become one, in love's perfect line.

Ribbons of Radiant Hopes

In morning's light, dreams take flight,
Bound by ribbons so bright.
Each whisper of hope, a gentle thread,
Winding paths where hearts are led.

Through valleys deep and mountains high,
Chasing visions across the sky.
With every step, a promise gleams,
Ribbons of love weave our dreams.

Even when shadows start to creep,
In steadfast faith, our spirits leap.
With every heartbeat, life unfolds,
In colors vibrant, stories told.

As twilight falls, we stand as one,
Underneath the setting sun.
Together we rise, never apart,
Ribbons of hope entwined in heart.

Symphony of Vulnerable Moments

In the silence, courage sings,
A symphony of fragile things.
Every tear a note we play,
In melodies of night and day.

Hands trembling, voices low,
Sharing secrets, letting go.
In vulnerable spaces, we unite,
Creating harmony in the night.

Each stumble gives the music depth,
A human song, each breath a step.
With open hearts, we learn to trust,
In awkward beauty, find the dust.

As dawn arrives, the song still lingers,
A tapestry woven with tender fingers.
In every heartbeat, a rhythm calls,
The symphony of life enthralls.

Elixir of Ephemeral Bliss

Moments fleeting like morning dew,
Whispered secrets shared by two.
In laughter's glow, joy ignites,
An elixir found in endless nights.

The world spins soft in twilight's hue,
As stars awaken, dreams come true.
In fragile whispers, love's embrace,
Ephemeral bliss we chase.

Through every smile, a memory we keep,
In fleeting glances, promises sweep.
With every heartbeat, life takes flight,
Finding magic in the night.

When dawn breaks, we hold it near,
The essence of joy, so clear.
In brief encounters, souls align,
Elixir of bliss, forever divine.

Journey Through Emotional Landscapes

Through valleys lush and mountains steep,
We wander where the wild hearts weep.
In fields of gold, our stories unfold,
Journeying forth, both brave and bold.

Waves of sorrow, tides of mirth,
In each turn, we discover worth.
With every sunset, colors blend,
Emotional landscapes never end.

Shadows dance on paths unknown,
In every step, new seeds are sown.
With open arms, we face the storms,
In every tempest, growth transforms.

As dawn brings light, we stand embraced,
In every moment, love interlaced.
Through the journey, we find our way,
Emotional landscapes guide our stay.

Fragments of Joy

In the morning light, whispers call,
A dance of shadows begins to sprawl.
Sun-kissed petals, laughter in bloom,
Each moment cherished, to fill the room.

A child's giggle, so pure and bright,
Tickling the heart, igniting the night.
Mirth in small things, a fleeting glance,
In fragments of joy, we find our stance.

Gentle rain falls, a soothing embrace,
Each drop a reminder, love's gentle trace.
In fleeting glimpses, our spirits soar,
Collecting the moments, we yearn for more.

Through shadows we navigate, hand in hand,
Together we journey, together we stand.
In fragments of joy, we weave our tale,
A tapestry rich, that will never pale.

Cascading Emotions

Like rivers that flow, feelings cascade,
In torrents of color, we find our shade.
From sorrow to laughter, we rise and fall,
Cascading emotions, the heart's own call.

A storm brews within, thunderous cries,
Yet tender moments can light up the skies.
A spark of hope in the darkest night,
Cascading emotions, our guiding light.

In layers we hide, shadows and dreams,
Yet honesty shines, brighter than beams.
Through heartache and healing, we learn to cope,
Cascading emotions, the essence of hope.

Every tear, every smile, fluid we share,
In this dance of feelings, nothing compares.
Let them flow freely, let them all show,
Cascading emotions, the beauty of glow.

The Art of Vulnerability

Beneath the armor, soft whispers speak,
In the art of vulnerability, we grow weak.
To bare our souls, a courageous feat,
In honesty's embrace, our hearts find heat.

The fragility of trust, a delicate thread,
Each stitch a promise, a path we tread.
In sharing our scars, we cultivate grace,
The art of vulnerability, a sacred space.

With open hearts, we journey as one,
In the light of truth, our shadows undone.
For strength can be found in the softest hearts,
The art of vulnerability, where healing starts.

Letting walls crumble, exposing the core,
In our shared stories, we open the door.
Through laughter and tears, we weave our song,
The art of vulnerability, together we belong.

A Kaleidoscope of Feelings

Swirls of colors, emotions collide,
In a kaleidoscope, we choose to reside.
From joyous laughter to deep, aching pain,
A dance of sensations, in sunshine and rain.

Patterns shift with every glance,
A luminous waltz, a vibrant romance.
In every twist, a new frame reveals,
A kaleidoscope of feelings, the heart's true deals.

Amidst the chaos, we find our way,
In the spectrum of life, we choose to stay.
With open arms, we embrace what's pure,
A kaleidoscope of feelings, that love endures.

In moments of silence, with echoes drawn near,
We unwrap our truths and face our fear.
Life's vivid mosaic, both tender and wild,
A kaleidoscope of feelings, forever beguiled.

Beyond the Horizon of Heartstrings

In silence, dreams take flight,
With whispers carried to the night.
We chase the stars, hand in hand,
A love that time cannot withstand.

Beyond the horizon, where souls unite,
Heartstrings woven, glowing bright.
Together we forge our sacred space,
Bound by an unbreakable embrace.

Each moment dances on the breeze,
In the warmth of our shared ease.
Through valleys deep, we wander far,
Guided by our morning star.

In the twilight's gentle sigh,
We let our spirits soar and fly.
Beyond the edge, where hopes ignite,
Our hearts entwined in endless light.

Dreamcatcher of Fleeting Emotions

In the night, dreams softly weave,
Emotions swirling, we believe.
Like whispers caught in silver thread,
A tapestry of words unsaid.

Through tangled fears, we find our way,
With each heartbeat, love's ballet.
Moments flicker like fireflies,
In the dance of truth, there are no lies.

Dreamcatcher glimmers in the dark,
Holding secrets of the heart's spark.
By morning light, all will be clear,
Fleeting shadows that do not adhere.

Emotions caught, like morning dew,
Hold them close, let them renew.
In every sigh, there's magic found,
With every heartbeat, love unbound.

Whispers of the Heart

In the stillness, whispers rise,
Softly spoken, no disguise.
Echoes brush against the soul,
Filling spaces, making whole.

With gentle strokes, the heart can feel,
Every truth that time reveals.
Between the lines of dreams and fears,
In spoken words, we shed our tears.

Cascading like a tranquil stream,
Whispers guide us through the dream.
In this symphony of light and sound,
Love's quiet pulse, forever found.

Let the whispers stir the night,
Illuminate with sweet delight.
In every sigh, a tale unfolds,
Heartfelt murmurs, pure as gold.

Embrace of Shadows

In twilight's arms, shadows meet,
Where silence dances softly, sweet.
Veils of dusk begin to fall,
In whispered tones, we hear the call.

Embrace the night, let go of fear,
In the darkness, love draws near.
With every heartbeat, soft and slow,
In shadows deep, our true selves show.

Beneath the stars, we find our way,
In the quiet, night turns to day.
Every secret, every sigh,
Shadows blend as we learn to fly.

Together we weave our fate anew,
In the embrace of night, we stay true.
Each moment a treasure, rich and vast,
In the arms of shadows, our love is cast.

Constellations of Inner Whispers

In the night, stars softly gleam,
Voices of secrets, a tender dream.
Each flicker a thought, a silent plea,
Guiding the heart to set it free.

Winds carry tales of old and new,
Beneath the vast sky, I feel the glue.
Whispers of hopes, woven in light,
Constellations dance, igniting the night.

In the stillness, truths often arise,
Embracing shadows, finding the skies.
Within the darkness, a spark ignites,
Inner echoes twine like velvet nights.

With every twirl, I trace my path,
Through cosmic dreams, escaping wrath.
In the quiet, I learn to see,
Constellations whispering, setting me free.

Threads of Time

Woven in moments, a fabric we share,
Each thread a story, a love laid bare.
Glistening memories, stitched with care,
In the tapestry of life, we declare.

Yesterday's echoes, tomorrow's grace,
Fleeting seconds, we cannot retrace.
Yet in this dance, we find our place,
Threads of emotion, time interlace.

Seasons unravel, yet we remain,
Bound by the joys, and also the pain.
Each heartbeat a rhythm, a sweet refrain,
Threads of connection, pulling the chain.

In the warp and the weft, our stories spun,
A journey together, never undone.
Through laughter and tears, every mile run,
Threads of time bind us, two into one.

Woven in Spirit

In every heartbeat, a tale unfolds,
Woven in spirit, a thread of gold.
Through laughter shared, and stories told,
A tapestry rich, each moment bold.

With every dawn, our spirits dance,
Intertwined like fate, in life's romance.
In whispers soft, we take our chance,
Woven in spirit, we find our stance.

Through storms and sun, our bond is strong,
In quiet corners, we both belong.
Each woven strand sings a joyful song,
In the circle of life, we carry on.

As stars align, our paths converge,
In the tapestry of life, love's urge.
Side by side, a sacred surge,
Woven in spirit, we both emerge.

Garden of Senses Awakened

In the garden where silence blooms,
Fragrant whispers, as nature looms.
Petals unfurl, revealing tunes,
Awakened senses beneath the moons.

Soft rustle speaks of twilight's grace,
Colorful blooms, a warm embrace.
Here every touch becomes a trace,
In this garden, I find my place.

With each gust of wind, stories sway,
Fingertips dance in a playful way.
In sunlight's kiss, I drift and play,
Garden of senses that guides my day.

Awakening dreams where spirits roam,
The heart finds peace, the soul a home.
In every blossom, wisdom's tome,
A garden of senses, where love is grown.

Labyrinth of Love's Echoes

In the maze where passion intertwines,
Echoes of laughter, sweet, divine.
Each turn unveils what softly shines,
Labyrinth of love, where heart aligns.

Through shadowed paths, emotions flow,
Winding secrets that softly glow.
In every heartbeat, whispers grow,
Love's echoes linger, ever so slow.

Entwined together, we lose our fears,
In a sacred space where time adheres.
With every moment, we shed our tears,
Labyrinth of love, where the heart steers.

Yet in this journey, we both shall find,
A tapestry rich, forever entwined.
In the depths of love, echoes remind,
Labyrinth of heart, both gentle and blind.

Bursts of Affection

Whispers flutter like wings of grace,
In shadows where soft moments trace.
Hearts collide with a gentle spark,
In the warmth of a fleeting lark.

Laughter dances in the air we breathe,
Wrapped in dreams that weaves and seethes.
Every glance a sparkling fire,
In an embrace that won't expire.

Time slows in this sacred space,
Where love unfolds, a tender lace.
The world fades, just you and I,
Under the canvas of the sky.

Bursting forth with colors bold,
Stories shared, and secrets told.
In a heart where affection blooms,
Life is bright with love's perfumes.

Uncharted Currents

Waves crash softly on distant shores,
Each whisper carries ancient roars.
In twilight's grip, the sea reveals,
Mysteries deep in swirling reels.

Guided by stars that brightly gleam,
We ride the tides of a wild dream.
A compass held by instinct's might,
Navigating the endless night.

Currents pull with a force unknown,
In waters where the wildness's grown.
Adventures wait in the deep blue,
Every moment feels fresh and new.

Boundless horizons whisper and call,
Echoes of freedom in each rise and fall.
Together we brave the distant sea,
On uncharted paths, just you and me.

Luminescent Echoes

Flickering lights in the midnight haze,
Illuminate thoughts in the quiet maze.
Every glow, a story to tell,
In the silence, our secrets dwell.

Voices drift like soft, gentle streams,
Carrying wishes, hopes, and dreams.
Each sparkle dances, inviting us near,
In the resonance of what we hold dear.

With every heartbeat, the night expands,
A symphony played by the stars' hands.
In luminous arcs, the moments fly,
Capturing time as we laugh and sigh.

Echoes linger in the starry dome,
In their embrace, we find our home.
With each breath, colors intertwine,
In the tapestry of love, divine.

Dances in Dusk

In the twilight, shadows softly sway,
Embracing the end of a vibrant day.
Leaves rustle to a whispered tune,
As stars awaken, one by one, soon.

A gentle breeze kisses the skin,
Pulling us close as the night begins.
With every step, we find our way,
In this ballet where dreams hold sway.

Under the blush of the setting sun,
We twirl in places where laughter's spun.
Time stands still, a beautiful ruse,
In the magic that dusk can infuse.

The world fades to an amber glow,
As darkness blankets the earth below.
In our hearts, the rhythms reside,
Dancing together, love as our guide.

A Garden of Gratitude

In the dawn's gentle light, we wake,
With hearts full of joy, no room for ache.
Each blossom a token, each leaf a song,
Nature whispers softly, you belong.

The dew-kissed petals, they shine anew,
Reminding us daily of all that is true.
With every small gesture, kindness does grow,
In this garden of gratitude, love does flow.

Sunlight cascades, warming the ground,
In the silence of beauty, peace can be found.
We nurture the roots, keep them held tight,
In this sacred space, we find our light.

As seasons may change, still we will tend,
To the flowers of hope, on which we depend.
In a garden where thanks forever reside,
We'll carry the love that will always abide.

Shadows Beneath the Surface

In whispers of twilight, secrets lie deep,
In the folds of the earth, where shadows creep.
Underneath the stillness, stories unfold,
Of dreams long forgotten, and truths left untold.

The river flows softly, with tales in its wake,
Beneath the calm surface, it starts to ache.
Ripples of silence, they shimmer and sway,
Inviting the brave to unveil the gray.

Through tangled branches, the moonlight will weave,
A tapestry woven with what we believe.
The heart is a mirror, reflecting the night,
In shadows we find, what brings forth the light.

Though fears may arise, let courage take hold,
Beneath all the shadows, there's treasure untold.
So dive into depths, where clarity swells,
In the quiet, discover the magic it tells.

A Veil of Wonder

In the still of the morning, a mist starts to rise,
With each breath we take, the world breathes in size.
Through the veil of the dawn, the colors ignite,
A symphony waking, the day from the night.

Each blossom a story, in petals they speak,
In the heart of the forest, where silence feels weak.
The wonders unfold as we wander along,
In the rustling leaves, we hear nature's song.

With eyes wide open, we dance on the breeze,
In every small moment, there's magic to seize.
Let wonder remind us to look and to find,
The beauty enfolded in the depths of our mind.

In a world wrapped in layers, so tender and bright,
May we seek the unseen, embrace the invite.
For beneath each horizon, new dreams can take flight,
In a veil of pure wonder, we find our delight.

The Beat of Being

In whispers of time, our hearts start to race,
Feeling the rhythm, in this sacred space.
Each moment a pulse, each breath a beat,
In the dance of existence, where joy and pain meet.

The syncopation of laughter, the echo of tears,
Weaving the fabric of all of our years.
In the tapestry woven, our essence resides,
In the pulse of our being, where true love abides.

With every small heartbeat, we learn, we belong,
In the symphony of life, a collective song.
The highs and the lows, together they blend,
In the beat of our being, we are never alone.

So cherish each heartbeat, let them be free,
In the echo of living, we find the harmony.
With open hearts anchored in now, we shall sing,
To the rhythm of life, the joy it can bring.

Starlit Whispers

In the quiet of the night,
Stars softly share their light.
Whispers travel on the breeze,
Carried far among the trees.

Underneath the velvet sky,
Moonlight dances as we sigh.
Dreams take flight on silver beams,
We are lost within our dreams.

Echoes linger, gently fade,
Memories in shadows shade.
Starlit paths we wander wide,
With each twinkle, hearts confide.

In the stillness, secrets bloom,
Casting off the weight of gloom.
Starlit whispers call our name,
Binding souls in cosmic flame.

Vortex of Sentience

Thoughts swirl like leaves in fall,
Spiraling through an endless call.
In this mind, a dance begins,
Life unravels, truth and sins.

Fractals of the heart entwined,
In the chaos, love defined.
Emotions twist, a vivid spree,
Vortex pulls us endlessly.

Each reflection, sharp and bright,
Daring us to face the light.
In this whirlwind, we will soar,
Through the tempest, seek for more.

With a blend of joy and pain,
Life's sweet symphony in rain.
Vortex of sentience alive,
In this swirl, our spirits thrive.

The Language of Longing

In a room without a name,
Whispers rise like gentle flame.
Silences stretch, horizons seem,
Hope entwined in every dream.

Eyes that speak the words untyped,
Hearts that beat with love unripe.
Every glance, a story told,
In the warmth, our souls enfold.

Through the distance, echoes call,
Filling spaces, breaking walls.
In the night, our hearts align,
With a rhythm so divine.

Longing binds us, thread by thread,
In the silence, truth is bred.
Language flows without a sound,
In this space, love's softly found.

Ripples of Resilience

Like stones cast in a stream,
Ripples form, and then we dream.
Each small wave a story told,
Strength emerges, brave and bold.

In life's waters, deep and wide,
We have learned to turn the tide.
Moments struggling through the strife,
Show us how to cherish life.

With the storms that come our way,
Hope endures with every day.
In the deep, we find our grace,
Ripples spread, and we embrace.

Through the trials, we will rise,
Strengthening beneath the skies.
Ripples of resilience shine,
In the heart, our spirits align.

Milton Keynes UK
Ingram Content Group UK Ltd.
UKHW030751121124
451094UK00013B/787

9 789916 907795